Why Should I Save for a Rainy Day?

Rachel Eagen

Crabtree Publishing Company
www.crabtreebooks.com

Author: Rachel Eagen

Series research and development: Reagan Miller

Editors: Reagan Miller and Janine Deschenes

Designer: Tammy McGarr

Photo research: Tammy McGarr and Crystal Sikkens

Proofreader: Crystal Sikkens

Prepress technician: Tammy McGarr

Print and production coordinator: Katherine Berti

Photographs
iStock: ?David Sacks: p 5; Rich Legg: p 14 (top right); Antonio_Diaz: p 19;

Shutterstock: © toeytoey: p 6

Superstock: © Hero Images Inc.: p 4;

Thinkstock: Keith Brofsky: p13; 3sbworld: p 15 (top left); Ryan McVay: p 20; Rachdole: p 21 (right)

All other images from Shutterstock

Library and Archives Canada Cataloguing in Publication

Eagen, Rachel, 1979-, author
Why should I save for a rainy day? / Rachel Eagen.

(Money sense : an introduction to financial literacy)
Includes index.
Issued in print and electronic formats.
ISBN 978-0-7787-2663-0 (hardback).--
ISBN 978-0-7787-2667-8 (paperback).--
ISBN 978-1-4271-1799-1 (html)

1. Finance, Personal--Juvenile literature. 2. Saving and investment--Juvenile literature. 3. Thriftiness--Juvenile literature. I. Title.

HG179.E222 2016 j332.024 C2016-904164-6
C2016-904165-4

Library of Congress Cataloging-in-Publication Data

CIP available at the Library of Congress

Crabtree Publishing Company

www.crabtreebooks.com 1-800-387-7650

Printed in Canada/082016/TL20160715

In Canada: We acknowledge the financial support of the Government of Canada through the Canada Book Fund for our publishing activities.

Published in Canada
Crabtree Publishing
616 Welland Ave.
St. Catharines, Ontario
L2M 5V6

Published in the United States
Crabtree Publishing
PMB 59051
350 Fifth Avenue, 59th Floor
New York, New York 10118

Published in the United Kingdom
Crabtree Publishing
Maritime House
Basin Road North, Hove
BN41 1WR

Published in Australia
Crabtree Publishing
3 Charles Street
Coburg North
VIC 3058

Table of Contents

What are Savings?

People use money to pay for their **needs** and **wants**. Needs are things that people must have to **survive**, or live. Needs include food, shelter, and clothing. Wants are things people would like to have, such as toys or a trip to the zoo.

People have to carefully plan how to use their money so that they have some left over to save.

Start saving!

When people have money left over after buying what they need, they can choose to **save** it. That means that they do not spend it. People may save money to buy needs and wants that cost a lot of money, such as a family vacation or college **tuition**. It can take a long time to save enough money to buy these kinds of needs and wants.

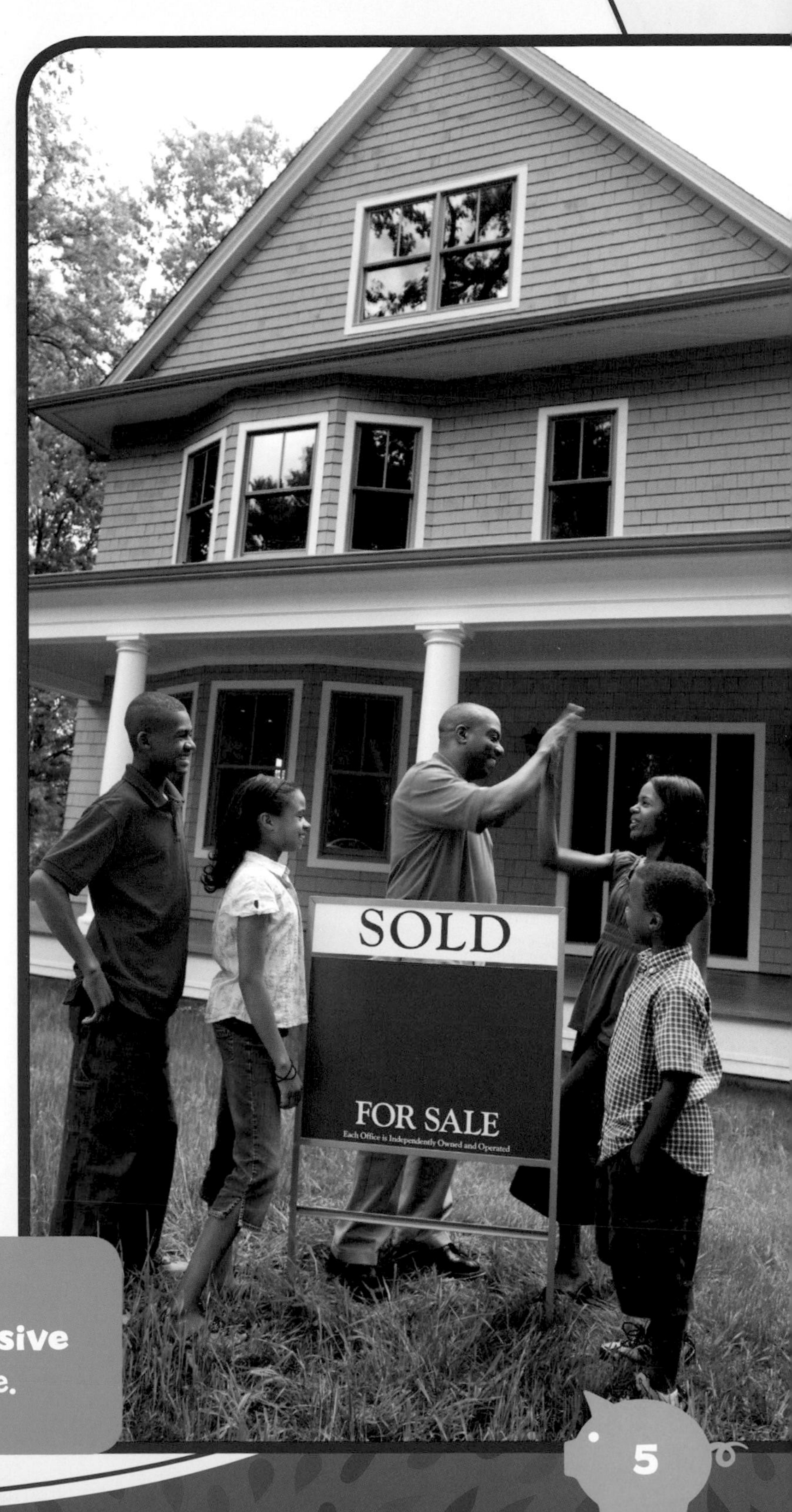

People need to save up a large amount of money to buy **expensive** wants and needs, such as a house.

Why Should I Save?

We do not have an unlimited supply of money. People **earn** money by working at their **jobs**. The money they earn is called their **income**. Then, they can spend their income on their wants and needs.

People work at jobs to afford the things they need and want. Parents earn money to afford the needs and wants of their families, too.

Long-term expenses are things that we don't need right away, but we will need in the future.

Spend or save?

People should not spend all of the money they earn. They need to save so that they can afford, or are able to buy, **long-term expenses**. Long-term expenses are things they will need in the future, such as a new car.

It all Adds Up!

Our wants and needs add up—which means that it can be hard to save money. Understanding the different types of expenses, or things we have to pay for, can help us make good spending and saving decisions.

You might have to decide whether to buy your lunch at school, or save your money and bring a lunch from home.

Expenses

There are three types of expenses. One has already been explained. Long-term expenses are things you will need in the future. **Short-term expenses** are things you will need soon, such as a new swimsuit for summer or a backpack for the start of the school year. **Fixed expenses** are things you always need to buy, such as groceries.

Make "cents" of it!

Look at the below list of the needs and wants of Olivia's family. Decide whether each expense is short-term, long-term, or fixed.

- **Olivia's cousin is getting married this month, and Olivia needs a new dress to wear to the wedding.**
- **Every month, Olivia's parents spend 100 dollars in gas for their car.**
- **Olivia's getting bigger. Soon her bike will be too small for her! She will need to buy a new one by next summer.**

Saving for the Unexpected

People have expenses that they can expect, and expenses that might take them by surprise. These surprise expenses are called **unexpected expenses**. Unexpected expenses are things people didn't expect to have to pay for, such as a car breaking down or replacing furniture that got damaged in a flood.

Having money saved for unexpected expenses makes tough situations a little easier to deal with.

The “what-if” fund

It’s important to save money for unexpected expenses. Some families call this money their “what-if” fund or their **emergency** fund. Without a “what-if” fund, it can be hard for people to afford their wants and needs if they have to suddenly pay for something unexpected.

Breaking an arm or leg can be an unexpected expense. Parents sometimes have to pay for doctor and hospital visits.

Where Do I Save?

Do you have a safe place for your money? Some kids keep money in a secret drawer or box. Others use piggy banks! It's important to keep your money safe.

A piggy bank is a good place to keep left over money. You will be surprised how much money a piggy bank can hold!

When people take money out of a bank account, it is called a **withdrawal**.

Money in the bank

Large amounts of money should be kept in **bank accounts**. Banks are businesses that keep money safe. They keep track of people's money for them. Adults use bank accounts to save their money. Putting money away in a bank account helps stop people from spending it.

How Do I Save?

Starting to save money early is a good choice. It may not seem like much, but putting even a small amount of money away now can make big changes in the future! Once you get in the **habit** of saving, it's easy!

Before you can save money, you have to make some! Some kids earn money by helping around the house or doing jobs for neighbors. Others get money as a gift for birthdays or other holidays.

A little makes a lot!

Saving a little money as often as you can adds up quickly! Think about ways you could spend less and save. Maybe you and your friends watch a movie at home, instead of going out to the movies. Or, maybe you bring lunch from home instead of buying it at school.

Handmade gifts are just as nice as gifts you can buy at the store. Making gifts instead of buying them is a good way to save money.

Make "cents" of it!

You can start saving now! Make a list of the things you usually spend your money on. You could include things like toys, books, food, or birthday gifts for friends and family. Ask an adult to help you figure out how much each thing costs. Then, think about ways that you could save. How much money could you save by making some changes?

Planning to Save

A **budget** is a plan for using money. People use budgets to figure out how much money they can spend on different wants and needs every day, week, month, year, or longer.

Sofia's Budget
Month: March

Money Earned		Money Spent	
Walking dog	$2.25	Comic book	$3.75
Paper route	$12.75	Movie night	$12.75
Birthday money from Grandma	$10.00	Buying lunch at school	$10.00
Total	$25.00	Total	$26. 50

Look at Sofia's budget. Did she earn or spend more in March? What could she do to improve or change her budget for the month of April?

Budget to save!

It's easy to save money when you know how much money you need to spend on your wants and needs. A budget can help you know how much money you will have left over. For example, you might figure out that you have one dollar left over from your allowance every week. Saving one dollar per week can help you buy that new bike or pair of skates you want!

Keeping track of how much money you are spending and saving is a good way to make sure you can buy all of your needs.

Debt

When people do not have enough money saved to buy expensive needs and wants, such as cars, they sometimes borrow money from banks or from other people. Borrowed money is called **debt**.

Large amounts of money borrowed to buy things such as a house may take a long time to pay back.

People sometimes borrow money using a **credit card**. At the end of each month, they have to pay back any money they spent using the card.

Paying it back

When you borrow money, you have to pay it back. When people borrow large amounts of money for big purchases they might pay back small amounts of their debt over a long period of time. Going into debt can be a problem. Sometimes, people cannot pay it back. It's better to make a plan to save your money, than to borrow it.

Your Turn!

Learning to save is an important money skill to have. Saving allows us to buy the things we will need or want in the future. Without savings, most people would not have money to pay for large or unexpected expenses.

Start saving when you are young and you will be surprised how much money you will have saved up when you grow up!

Planning for the future

Do you have your eye on a new toy or game? What happens if your shoelaces break, or you drop your new iPod in the pool? Even kids like you need savings! Every bit counts.

Make "cents" of it!

Imagine you are paid $20 for helping your neighbor rake leaves in the fall. Will you save it, or choose to spend it? What will you buy with it?

Make a list of the different things you could do with the money. Then, make the best decision. Share your reasons for spending or saving with a friend.

Learning More

Books

Drobot, Eve. *Money Money Money: Where It Comes From, How to Save It, Spend It, and Make It*. Toronto: Maple Tree Press Inc. 2004.

Hall, Margaret. *Money: Earning, Saving, Spending*. Chicago: Heinemann. 2008.

Vermond, Kira. *The Secret Life of Money: A Kid's Guide to Cash*. Toronto: Owlkids Books Inc. 201.

Websites

Kids.gov
https://kids.usa.gov/money/saving-money/index.shtml

Rich Kid Smart Kid
www.richkidsmartkid.com

The Mint
www.themint.org

Three Jars
www.threejars.com

Words to Know

Note: Some boldfaced words are defined where they appear in the book.

bank account (bangk uh-KOUNT) noun A record of money held at a bank for safe keeping

budget (BUH-it) noun A plan for using money

credit card (KRED-it kahrd) noun A card that allows a person to make purchases right away and pay for them later

debt (det) noun Borrowed money that must be paid back

earn (urn) verb To gain by working

emergency (ih-MUR-juh n-see) noun Something that happens unexpectedly and needs attention right away

expensive (ik-SPEN-siv) adjective Very high-priced

habit (HAB-it) noun A pattern or routine done regularly and often without even thinking about it

income (IN-kuhm) noun Money received for doing jobs

job (job) noun A task done for a set amount of money

save (seyv) verb To keep or avoid spending

tuition (too-ISH-uh n) noun The amount of money charged by a school for teaching

A noun is a person, place, or thing.

A verb is an action word that tells you what someone or something does.

An adjective is a word that tells you what something is like.

Index

About the Author

Rachel Eagen studied Creative Writing and English Literature at university. Now, she edits and writes books for a living. She is the author of 19 other books for children and youth. She once saved her allowance for a year, and then spent it all on gummi bears.